THE SECRET

PR(

Louie Morley

CONTENTS

The 5AM CLUB

What do a businessman, an artist, and a billionaire have in common? Each of them rises at five in the morning. The 5 AM Club (2018) will show you how to alter your morning, take back control of your life, and derive more personal growth and zeal from your first hour of the day than the majority of individuals do over the entire week. Though it may seem impossible, you may learn how to do it by following their journey.

Introduction

What is the secret to becoming a billionaire? There must be one because if everyone knew how to go there, they would all have billions of dollars by now. The truth is that everyone pursues their goals using a variety of tactics; there is no one recipe for success.

One extremely affluent billionaire used this approach to start his day at five in the morning. In fact, he was so confident in this strategy that he attributed all of his success to it rather than to his natural business acumen or the time he had invested in his company.

Lucky for you, it's not a secret! In this short, we'll learn how to join what he called "the 5 a.m club" and why it might change your life. Even more fascinating information will be covered, including the importance of brain relaxation, the benefits of rising early, and the characteristics of a successful morning routine.

CHAPTER 1: THE 5 A.M CLUB

For the purposes of this summary, imagine a group of people whose roles are similar to those of The Breakfast Club members. A businessman who thinks his life is pointless is present. An artist who has lost hope is making an effort to ignite their creative spark. Not to mention, we also have a crazy billionaire coach who can offer some unconventional success advice.

Imagine that they all attend a business conference where "The Spellbinder," a well-known business expert known for his ability to "wow" audiences and impart insightful success advice, will be the keynote speaker.

After the keynote talk, the billionaire approaches our business owner and artist in disguise. He wasn't dressed like a millionaire; in fact, his attire was horribly inadequate. He frequently wore clothing that suggested he was in dire need in order to demonstrate to himself and others that wealth isn't everything and that one shouldn't judge someone's worth or wealth only based on their appearance.

This, though, was also a deliberate tactic. When he explained that the Spellbinder was actually his personal tutor and that he had made a fortune by heeding his advice, you can only imagine how shocked the other party members were. The two, already fascinated, listened as he explained how the Spellbinder had taught him that, despite the fact that many people desire extraordinary events to take place for them, truly admirable people are aware of their capacity to bring about such extraordinary events.

He told them that one tip—more important than anything else—held the key to a remarkable future, and they were curious to find out what it was. When he revealed that developing "a world-beating morning routine" was the solution, they were even more shocked. But when the millionaire offered to teach them everything he knew the following day as long as they saw him at 5 a.m., they jumped at the chance. And so their journey began.

CHAPTER 2: ELITE PERFORMERS GET UP AT 5 AM

Our entrepreneur and artist, like most of us, weren't used to getting up so early, so they listened groggily as their new teacher described how getting up at five in the morning had helped him escape the mediocrity that so easily ensnares people.

Additionally, he informed them that many notable figures, such as Mozart and John Grisham, were able to convert their output and excel in their fields by rising at this hour!

Here's how it works:

We all have a daily mental energy budget; you could think of your mental energy as your cognitive capacity. Numerous sources fight daily for your attention by utilizing your meager bandwidth.

Everything demands your attention as soon as you get out of bed, including your work and relationships as well as the news and the internet. These continual pressures that make us feel compelled to multi-task and move our focus between numerous things seriously impair our ability to consistently focus on one thing.

However, by lunchtime, we've already been so overwhelmed with requests that it's difficult to focus on anything. But rising at five in the morning literally fires up your brain, enabling you to focus as much as you can!

You may blame transient hypofrontality for anything. Simply expressed, this means that when you rise at 5 a.m., your pre-frontal cortex, which regulates logical reasoning, temporarily suffers. If, like me, you typically start your day being tormented by anxiety, doubts, and fears, then one advantage of getting up at five in the morning is the ability to temporarily mute them. The creation of dopamine and serotonin is pre-programmed to increase at this time of day, which will make you joyful and give you a more peaceful start to the day.

Therefore, it stands to reason that when you eliminate unimportant thoughts and self-criticism and replace them with energy, tranquility, and productivity, you'll naturally reach a state of flow in which you're happier and more focused.

The opportunities are infinite if you start each day with that kind of enthusiasm! You might also want to consider the fact that in order to perform at your absolute best and rank among the top 5% of the world's elite performers, you must be willing to make sacrifices that the other 95% of people on the planet are not. If that isn't enough to convince you to give up a few hours of sleep each night.

And most individuals don't look forward to getting up at five in the morning. So if you want to get a major competitive advantage, this is a great method to learn!

CHAPTER 3: HOW TO BE A HISTORYMAKER

There are people who are successful, and there are people who make history and become well-known figures. The last category includes of people whose accomplishments are so significant that they render them eternal. They break records, push boundaries, and make contributions that are unimaginably significant. How do they differ, though? And what influences the level of success you have? Our rich coach believes that a history maker concentrates on these four areas.

One is their ability to maximize their talents. They may not be the most talented people, but they use their skills to the fullest. Instead of comparing your abilities to those of others and assuming you lack them, make the most of the capabilities you already have and use them to change the world. The second key area of focus is the ability to avoid being distracted. This is crucial because it's probably the primary obstacle preventing people from progressing.

And if you want to succeed, none of these distractions—such as a smartphone addiction or a debilitating relationship—can persist in your life. Concentration, focus, and simplification are crucial for creating a successful worldview.

Start by giving up multitasking and embracing a purist lifestyle where you concentrate only on a few crucial tasks rather than overstuffing your day with several small tasks. Eliminating distractions is also crucial, so approach the mental clutter in your life like a spring cleaning task! Turn off alerts when they are obstructing your focus. Get rid of things in your life that don't make you happy or add value. Join the 5 a.m. club to give yourself an uninterrupted hour to start your day, and that's most important!

Third, it's important to understand how day-stacking works. Day-stacking is the concept that accomplishing a few small things consistently is more important than doing a few big things sometimes.

Therefore, concentrate on gradually developing one small gift or skill each day! If you want to manage your email inbox, create a better daily plan, or increase your productivity in a few specific areas, this is the best technique to employ. The final key area of focus for history creators is the practice of personal mastery.

This idea is based on psychologist Anders Ericsson's theory that mastering a skill at an elite level requires 2.75 hours of actual practice. Therefore, if you want to actually master yourself and get the ability to create a profitable future, set aside the first two to three hours of each day to concentrate intently on increasing your self-awareness, thinking, and attitude.

CHAPTER 4: YOUR FOUR INTERIOR EMPIRES

If you've ever attended a business conference, it's probable that you frequently heard tips on how to sharpen your thinking, just like our entrepreneur and artist did. The millionaire did, however, acknowledge that the attitude is just one of four internal empires that require constant attention and growth! It's great to work on your mindset, but if that's all you do, your Heartset, Healthset, and Soulset are being neglected!

So let's look at each of these categories and how they affect your life.

Your "heartset," as you may have heard it called, is exactly what it sounds like it is. Since each of your four inner empires is interconnected, it doesn't matter how strong and healthy your Mindset is if your Heartset is in disorder. Furthermore, Sigmund Freud, while being widely ridiculed, was right when he asserted that "Unexpressed emotions will never die." They are still alive, and they will later reappear in ever more horrifying ways.

When you consider that reality and the impact that emotional instability may have on your life, the conclusion that improving your emotional well-being paves the way for a happier, more stable existence overall follows naturally.

Your Healthset is essential since, as you might anticipate, having poor health greatly limits your capacity to perform tasks. Make a commitment to your bright future by taking good care of yourself now, and make a commitment to exercise to improve your health and productivity. Despite the fact that the physical and emotional benefits of exercise are well-documented, it doesn't hurt to be aware that exercise may boost the flow of good hormones and lessen stress, both of which may be highly advantageous to your personal and professional lives.

Not to mention, it's crucial that you focus on your Soulset as well. As your spirituality or balancing force, think about your Soulset. By focusing on your Soulset, you'll be able to connect with your true self and sever your ties to the transient and pointless components of daily life. Getting up at five in the morning can help with this as well because it will give you time for reflection on what you can contribute to society.

CHAPTER 5: THE 20/20/20 FORMULA

Now that we are aware of our four inner empires, let's examine some practical, everyday strategies for expanding them. Since nothing could be further from the truth despite the fact that getting up at five in the morning may appear like a miracle treatment. Until you use it to be proactive and take specific measures toward better yourself, 5 A.M. won't be any different from any other time you may wake up. As you would have expected, the genuine magic lies in how you use that time.

And the most effective technique to increase productivity is to use the 20/20/20 strategy made famous by the millionaire.

Using the premise that you should use 20 minutes for exercise, 20 minutes for reflection, and 20 minutes for growth, this plan helps you develop each of your four inner empires for a good start to your day.

As a result, start by exercising vigorously for 20 minutes. Remember what we spoke earlier about how your brain is clear and stress-free at this time. I know that's probably the last thing you want to do at 5:00 in the morning. The nicest part is that if you can get up at five in the morning, you'll kind of have a chance to surprise your brain before it becomes enough awake to inform you that exercising at five in the morning isn't really your thing. So, take advantage of that opportunity by concentrating on moving quickly enough to actually start perspiring.

You should pay specific attention to perspiring because it releases the protein BDNF, which promotes the growth of new synaptic connections and lowers the level of cortisol, also known as the "fear hormone," in your brain.

This suggests that even just 20 minutes of intensive exercise may help you develop faster thinking skills, boosting your everyday productivity. When you're done, spend the brief window of time between 5:20 and 5:40 A.M. alone and reflecting.

Before your day is filled with conflicting demands and diversions, take a moment to reflect on what matters most to you. Put your attention on your main worries during this period of reflection.

After reflecting for about ten minutes, spend the following ten minutes writing down your thoughts in a journal. Keep a journal to keep track of your objectives, worries, gripes, and blessings.

Imagine releasing these stresses from your own heart and mind while you do this, and transferring them to the paper. When you're finished writing, meditate for the brief time that remains. According to studies, if you begin your day with two activities that reduce your fear hormones—meditation and exercise—you'll have a double brave start to the day.

By thinking on the new insights you've gained from your reflection and writing, you could also feel more at ease and in charge. This tranquility will follow you for the remainder of the day.

Use the first hour of your morning right now, the last 20 minutes. Study during these 20 minutes because now is the time for growth. Whether you want to read a biography, listen to a podcast that promotes thought, or learn something new about marketing, economics, or innovation, you may tailor your learning experience to the interests that will benefit you and your career the most.

Decide to dedicate 20 minutes a day to your pursuit of knowledge because every great person in history was also known for their love of learning and commitment to personal growth.

So there you have it! This method not only provides you with a pre-made ideal morning routine, but it also shows you how to unlock the full potential of each and every 5 A.M. club member.

CHAPTER 6: EMBRACE SLEEP

in the early morning, about five. It certainly doesn't seem like a system that values sleep, but using the 5 A.M. requires a good night's sleep. group to produce life-altering results!

The millionaire told his new proteges that studies have revealed that sleep is one of the major factors at play when it comes to determining life expectancy. How you spend your final hour of the day is equally as significant as how you spend your first hour.

If we are anything like the majority of people, we are all sleep deprived these days, whether we are working professionals, students, or parents. According to studies, technology is primarily to blame for our inability to get enough shut-eye. In particular, our favorite devices to use before bed, such as phones and TVs, produce blue lights that inhibit the creation of melatonin, the hormone that promotes sleep.

Hence, turning off all gadgets at 8 o'clock. is advised by experts in sleep research in order to develop healthy sleep patterns. You'll be able to sleep better and get up at five in the morning by doing this. felt totally revived! But there are other ways to regain your energy than sleeping. Another great strategy the millionaire advises for improving performance is the twin-cycle of elite performance.

Here's how it works: instead of wearing yourself out with lengthy times of frenzied effort when you try to do everything that needs to be done, alternate between moments of intensive labor and profound refreshment to bring balance to your life. In order to maximize your potential and maintain good mental health, you must consciously schedule time for pleasure in addition to work.

Furthermore, by actively working to look after yourself, you lessen the possibility of burning out and offer yourself a chance to grow in both the performance phase and the recuperation phase.

But some of us might have a hard time accepting it. People with a "all work, no play" mentality, like our fictitious entrepreneur, could find it challenging to unwind and unwind.

We could even feel guilty when we aren't working, as though we are squandering our time on unnecessary things. But if we never lose sight of the significance of caring for our inner selves, we will be able to see the significance of balance and develop a healthy way of life.

CHAPTER 7: FINAL SUMMARY

It's crucial to take charge of your morning if you want to achieve your full potential for the remainder of the day. To boost your creativity and productivity, make it a habit to rise at 5 AM every day and spend the first hour of your day practicing the 20/20/20 method.

If you alter your way of thinking, you can succeed. When we observe people who appear to have their lives in order and who appear to achieve in all they undertake, it is easy to assume that success must be a trait that some people possess and others do not.

HOW

SUCCESFUL PEOPLE THINK

If you alter your way of thinking, you can succeed. When we observe people who appear to have their lives in order and who appear to achieve in all they undertake, it is easy to assume that success must be a trait that some people possess and others do not.

INTRODUCTION

Do you ever have the feeling that you are sleeping through life? It's easy to wonder where the day went and what you accomplished with it after going through the rituals of waking up, going to work, eating, and sleeping.

The most depressing aspect of this pattern's continued repetition for the bulk of us is that it appears to be in an endless loop. Have you finished it yet? Do you ever ponder how other circumstances might have affected your life? Imagine you had a job you enjoyed.

If any of these feelings sound familiar to you, there needs to be a significant adjustment. Now is the time to feel as prepared and recharged as when your phone is fully charged.

This overview will look at the mindset that drives the actions of all successful people as well as how to adopt this mindset in your own life.

CHAPTER 1: CULTIVATE BIG PICTURE THINKING

What would you say best describes the attitude you start each day with? Do you think that when you begin a task, "I'm going to be good at my work" or "I'm going to grow in my profession" come first to mind? Are you thinking about how to get through the day? Or do you consider how your actions today might impact your future?

Think carefully about which of these two categories best represents your general outlook on life, as most people firmly fall into one of them. Even if you don't agree with the answers, the truth is that it will determine your success both now and in the future!

This is because someone with a "be good" mentality only wants to show that he can handle the specifics of his profession as required. He doesn't really care about growing himself or picking up new talents; all he really wants is to excel in his current job, or maybe even just perform okay. And doing that won't help you advance in life.

You're more likely to keep working at the same unsatisfying job repeatedly. That way of thinking won't get you very far, and to make matters worse, it will make you feel that your life has no true significance or purpose. No one wants to live like that! A person who works hard to succeed is constantly looking for new opportunities to succeed and give their best effort.

A person with this mentality constantly assesses his performance against what he accomplished yesterday and wonders if he has improved.

Today, far from content with his current situation. This is yet another distinguishing trait of successful people's cognitive processes: comparing yourself to others is very different from evaluating your growth against your own personal best.

Comparing yourself to your coworkers could result in minor worries and concerns that are easy to get sucked into. It's easy to spend a lot of time questioning if you can match Suzie from Marketing in terms of IQ, talent, or likelihood of getting a promotion. A successful person is aware that it is never beneficial to compare oneself to others, nevertheless.

Since Suzie's achievement has no bearing on your own potential, value, or worth, a successful person is aware that it will not effect your own success. You don't wish to surpass anyone else, which is why. Your goal is not to be better than other people. Becoming the best version of yourself should be your goal. Therefore, the successful person prioritizes their own growth and views challenges as opportunities for growth rather than comparing themselves to others or being discouraged by failures.

The best part is that since the human brain is so adaptable, you can change your "be good" mentality to "get better" if that makes sense to you. It's quite easy to teach yourself to develop better habits!

Start by letting go of your fear of making mistakes, and you'll see how. We're all a little bit afraid of seeming foolish or messing up, despite the fact that studies have shown that the most successful people are those who freely and honestly disclose their propensity for making mistakes. And because they no longer experience the paralyzing anxiety that frequently causes people to make careless errors, they actually have a lower chance of making mistakes.

It's a good habit to get in the practice of asking for help. Because we want to appear as though we have everything under control and can handle anything, we frequently find it difficult to ask for help.

Figuring it all out on our own. The answer to this problem is as straightforward as "Stop being afraid to appear ignorant!"

If your objective is to progress in both your professional and personal lives, you'll realize that ignorance is an opportunity to learn. Because they probably won't mind you learning from them, don't be afraid to ask for assistance from others.

CHAPTER 2: NEVER STOP LEARNING

Success depends on learning, as you presumably inferred from the previous chapter!

This entire chapter is devoted to discussing the benefits of learning as a result. Successful people are aware that success necessitates constant adaptability. because as you tweak, you learn what works and what doesn't. You gain the capacity to reject unfavorable attitudes and poor habits and concentrate on favorable ones. Therefore, if you want to succeed, we'll go over some of the most important principles in more detail in this chapter.

The author claims that the capacity for creative thought is one of the really crucial elements for anyone's achievement. You must think creatively if you want to progress yourself, regardless of your goals or the industry you work in.

However, it can be one of the hardest mindsets to cultivate. This explains why we spend the first eighteen years of our lives learning how to blend in with society. For instance, we learn to respect others' speech by remaining silent throughout it. We are instructed not to be arrogant, boastful, or gossipy. And as a result of this training, we frequently allow others' ideas and accomplishments to transcend our own.

But the author makes clear that this can occasionally be harmful to us. Because it's important to be considerate and nice, to know when to hold your tongue and when to speak up. To put it another way, we must understand when to support the status quo and when to criticize it.

Knowing when to complete such tasks is critical from a business perspective. Because if you are unable to think outside the box, you may miss out on many opportunities that require inventive thinking.

Let's imagine that your company is working to create the next big thing in terms of a product. You need to think of something that will outshine your competitors and spread across the country. (Really, there's no pressure. A concept like that might be difficult to come up with, especially if you aren't capable of critical and creative thought. It can be easy to give in under such strain and avoid from trying anything new.

After all, mistakes do happen. There's a chance that your suggestion won't be well received. And each of those options is a strong contender. You may be sure that someone else will succeed before you if you never give it a go. Because you might have come up with a wonderful concept even though you may have had a few stupid ones along the way!

But unless you do it, you won't know. And you'll never win over those who do continue, who don't give up when things get tough, and who put in endless hours to develop their brilliant ideas. As a result, your business will probably eventually become obsolete.

No one desires that! And because of this, the author argues, we need an attitude shift. If we want to succeed in the always changing business world, we will have to completely redesign our cognitive processes. And doing so requires learning new viewpoints and strategies. Although it may be difficult to entirely alter one's perspective, the author believes that doing so is crucial for survival.

The author argues that in order to develop that new perspective, you must first learn to control your emotions. People are naturally afraid of strange things. It is because of this defense mechanism that we have survived and evolved. Although this may have benefited our caveman predecessors, it frequently leads to our present-day reluctance to try new things.

We tend to be afraid of the unknown, which keeps us from taking chances.

We worry that we'll mess up, fail, or come off as stupid. In some circumstances, our fear keeps us from attempting anything novel at all. Therefore, you must learn to control your emotions if you truly want to learn new things.

So, what is your procedure? The first step is to acknowledge that failure could present an opportunity. Since nobody wants to fail or admit that they made a mistake, we frequently view failure as the worst possible outcome in any situation. But failure actually gives you a chance to learn! We have the chance to get better every time we do something wrong.

In this way, we can start the learning process by letting go of our fear and viewing failure as a chance.

CHAPTER 3: SUCCESSFUL PEOPLE GET THEIR PRIORITIES IN ORDER

Do you ever have the feeling that your to-do lists are actually just lists of lists? Or do your plans, organizers, and productivity tools make you feel overburdened? You buy them because you think that if you have the right tools at your disposal, you can control your life and become more productive.

Unfortunately, you already know that it doesn't work like that. Since each of those items is merely a tool, They are helpful instruments that you can utilize, just like a tire gauge can help you with tire repair. However, unlike a tire gauge, they are unable to take immediate action and improve your life. Never will you check items off of your to-do list while you are asleep in your planner.

Unfortunately, until you put in the effort, these tools won't help you. However, it's frequently easier to say than to do.

In the digital age, there are more distractions than ever and our attention spans are shorter than ever. It could seem challenging to finish one task while remaining on course. The same is true in terms of self-incentivizing. Sure, you could tell yourself, "Get this done and then you can have a cupcake," but we all know that you could just eat the cupcake right away, whether or not you finish the assignment.

So how do you actually do it? How do you develop a plan, stick to it, and actually accomplish your goals? Setting priorities for your chores is, in the author's opinion, the first step to living your greatest, finest, and most fruitful life.

The fast-paced nature of modern life makes it simple to forget to plan ahead because it seems that your assignment for the upcoming week or year will be over in the blink of an eye. Pozen, though, believes that planning is crucial if you want to manage your calendar as opposed to letting it run you over.

So how can you plan effectively? A great strategy is to categorize and organize all of the many tasks you're getting ready for. Planning a career transition is very different from, say, scheduling the board meeting for next week. As a result, the author advises organizing your plans into categories based on "aims," "objectives," and "targets." You can think of "aims" as important, all-encompassing objectives with regard to your job.

For instance, you may plan your strategy over a number of years if your goal was to create a new branch of your business. Therefore, a goal is extremely dissimilar from an objective, which might be finished in a few months or years. Establishing an internship program at your company is a great goal. Finally, objectives are shorter, more immediate activities.

Targets are more urgent goals because they often take less than two months to fulfill, such as finalizing your paperwork or developing an advertising campaign. Additionally, it's imperative that you maintain track of and organize your goals because they're more likely to become a part of your everyday activities.

For instance, if you have a lot of work to do, think about making choices that will allow you to break it up into smaller, more manageable chunks. Imagine you have to read a 50-page paper and then make a PowerPoint presentation using the information you learned. It appears overwhelming when you consider that assignment as a whole. Hours will be required! It's enough to persuade you to give up and start binge-watching your preferred Netflix series.

But what if you broke that enormous task down into smaller parts and handled each one separately? Start by mentally reordering your assignment and reminding yourself, "I need to read this paper first," as an example. If you can do this in a quiet workspace, perhaps with a cup of savory coffee or tea for a dose of tasty encouragement, it's easier to focus on one task at a time.

Treat yourself to a short break or a cupcake after accomplishing that task before going on to the next.

CHAPTER 4: FINAL SUMMARY

The famous quote by writer Charles Swindoll goes, "I am persuaded that life is 10% what occurs to us and 90% how we react to it." The same might be said of our success plan.

It's easy to think that certain people are just more talented than others, but the author claims that this is completely wrong. Instead, the secret to success is in your thinking. Therefore, all you need to do to increase your success is to develop proper thinking skills.

The beautiful thing is that cultivating a success mindset is actually rather easy. All you have to do is prioritize your goals correctly, allow yourself to make mistakes, never stop learning, and engage in big-picture thinking. That is all there is to it!

THE 10X RULE

By GRANT CARDONE

Years have gone into perfecting Grant Cardone's recipe for success. Based on his expertise as a successful business owner and sales trainer, Cardone offers practical suggestions for achieving even the most ambitious goals. With the 10X Rule, you'll learn what it takes to succeed and how one straightforward idea can help you accomplish goals that previously seemed impossible.

INTRODUCTION

If you want to change your life, you should read this book. Everyone who wishes to succeed should follow the 10X Rule. It will ensure that you keep this style of thinking throughout your life and career in addition to teaching you how to act and think in a way that promotes success.

Your life, goals, and dreams will be revitalized by applying the 10X rule, which will help you be more courageous and less afraid.

This strategy has been tried and tested and is successful, despite the fact that it could appear too good to be true. Grant Cardone's many years of accomplishment led him to the discovery of the 10X rule as the secret to success.

It will show you how to create the right goals, estimate the necessary effort, learn how to approach your duties with the right attitude, and finally decide how much activity to undertake.

But you shouldn't be here if you're one of those people who thinks success will just happen to you by accident. The 10X rule is for people who have the determination to work hard and are willing to dedicate themselves to what it takes to succeed.

The good news is that the 10X rule doesn't discriminate and can ensure your success no matter your skill level, degree of education, financial situation, time management skills, industry, or level of luck. Once you begin to apply this advice to your own life, you'll be able to perform at levels you never thought possible.

CHAPTER 1: HOW THE 10X RULE WORKS

People wait their entire lives for success to "fall into their laps" because they think that success will come to those who wait it out. But as any successful person will tell you, it requires grit and tenacity. There are many ways to locate it, but Grant Cardone has devoted his life to figuring out a reliable path. Here, the 10X rule comes into play.

The 10X mentality states that you should put forth ten times as much effort as those around you. No matter how difficult it may appear at first, if you aren't willing to put in the extra effort, you won't be able to stand out from your peers. Cardone would, for instance, establish a goal of making 10 calls for each one his teammate made.

By establishing this goal instead of his colleague, he was putting himself in front of ten times as many clients. This tactic ultimately led to a promotion because it showed his boss and clients that he was a persistent and motivated individual.

The 10X rule, however, goes beyond merely attempting. The second half of the advice is to set goals that are 10 times more ambitious than what is considered feasible. When people set goals, they typically pick ones that are realistic and that they are confident they can achieve.

Although setting these goals may seem sensible, doing so will prevent you from moving forward.

Your initial impression may be that your goals are unreachable, but that's the point! As you raise your goals, you become more eager to put in more effort to reach them. Furthermore, you don't feel as upset when you fail to achieve a difficult goal as you do when you fail to achieve a weak one, isn't that right? Make your goal to save $1,000,000 if your goal is to save $100,000, for example.

At least once per day, after giving them some thought, write down your aspirational goals. Yes, that's right, once a day. Most people simply write down their goals once a year, which is a wonderful start but doesn't keep your goals at the forefront of your mind.

If you write down your goals once a day, you'll make them more concrete in your mind and have a better chance of sticking to your strategy to achieve them.

CHAPTER 2: SUCCESS IS UNLIMITED

When beginning a new project, people frequently underestimate the amount of work needed to finish it. This behavior is typical, as Cardone himself had before erred. The most important thing to do in this situation is to keep a positive attitude and remind yourself that everything is possible.

You know, when faced with difficult work, people frequently adopt a "quitting" mindset; nevertheless, if you follow the 10X rule, you'll be prepared for even the most difficult assignments.

The 10X rule emphasizes the importance of being prepared to deal with any challenges that may emerge. Imagine you are launching a new product and you want to sell 100,000 units but your competitors only want to sell 10,000. If you decide to buy 100,000 items, you will be able to fill a lot of orders because you are ready to handle the huge capacity.

Many others would fail in this situation because they had not planned for a sizable influx of orders.

The 10X rule calls for you to approach achievement with the mindset that there can be enough success for everyone. In contrast to the widespread misconception that success is a goal, the 10X rule suggests realizing that achievement is continuous and boundless.

There is room in the world for many successful people; success is not a finite resource that will eventually run out. Some individuals believe that if you succeed, someone else must fail. But this isn't always the case. Instead, everyone has the ability to succeed as long as they put up the effort and work to achieve it.

Not only is success attainable, but it is also necessary. Success will not just happen to knock on your door, as was previously stated.

Cardone, on the other hand, had some time to process this reality.

For instance, when he was 25 years old, Cardone's life was dominated by drugs and partying. He was living aimlessly and without a purpose. One day he suddenly recognized that his unstable existence made his way of life untenable and unsatisfying. After that day, Cardone adopted a new viewpoint on his work in sales and began putting more effort into becoming the best in the industry.

Cardone experienced a second epiphany about achievement when he was 50 years old. He realized that he was getting too comfortable in life and that he needed to keep striving for success if he wanted to lead a fulfilling life.

After that, Cardone adopted a 10X approach in all aspects of his life. For instance, Cardone and his wife saw it as both an honor and a responsibility to be the best parents to their children. It also includes never giving up on your pursuit of success.

CHAPTER 4: DON'T SETTLE FOR AVERAGE

When you hear the word "average," you might think of comfort or perhaps getting by. You might think of yourself as average.

working a normal amount of hours, making a normal amount of money, and doing a normal range of things.

Cardone, though, considers it dangerous to be average. He still refers to it as the "ordinary epidemic" despite this. Doing an ordinary work will result in failure, but why? The truth is that as the American economy shifts toward technology, those with mediocre employment are most susceptible to changes in the market's workforce, which could have severe consequences.

But according to the 10X rule, you shouldn't accept mediocrity in any area of your life. If you aren't prepared for an expensive catastrophe, accepting a conventional bank account runs the risk of leaving you in financial ruin.

Avoid falling into the trap of believing that being average is good enough; if you do, you'll never succeed. Aiming for a middle-class lifestyle is dangerous, to put it mildly.

In spite of the fact that the typical middle-class income in the US is between $35,000 and $50,000, it is just insufficient when compared to some of the "greatest cities" in the nation, such New York or Los Angeles. Instead, you need to get out there and do something constructive to give up your "middle-class mentality."

So many people in the middle class spend their leisure time watching TV or using social media because they are happy with their lifestyles. Cardone refers to this as the "middle-class squeeze."

A squeeze occurs when the cost of living increases but middle-class salaries do not. The upper class is less impacted by this burden due to their absence from the workforce and the fact that they get government aid.

Being in the middle class during a recession is perilous because in the end, middle-class households suffer the most. Cardone advises aiming for extraordinary or middle-class status as opposed to setting high standards and moving beyond being adequate.

CHAPTER 5: BECOME OBSESSIVE

Obsessive people are frequently linked to negative traits, such as someone who obsessively pursues an ex-lover. On the other hand, Cardone claims that when you become obsessed on something, like success, nothing can go wrong! Actually, if you become obsessed with your objective, you have a much higher probability of achieving it. The best way to build an obsession is to give it your all.

Despite the fact that you might not know it, going all in is risky. Consider engaging in a poker hand. Going all-in has two possible outcomes: either you win it all or you lose it all. Thankfully, life is less perilous than a round of poker.

Cardone is arguing that if you truly commit to your ideas, you will put in the necessary time and energy to make them a reality. For instance, if you want to start a business, be prepared to overcommit. Spend all of your time and energy finding new consumers and making sales. Send as many emails as necessary, post on social media frequently, and call as often as necessary. Repeat the process once everything has been finished.

Before you overcommit, you must define what your goals are. Make sure your goals are difficult enough to motivate you to work toward them. To do this, select challenges that seem nearly insurmountable and truly commit to them; to do this, you'll need to be imaginative and think imaginatively to come up with solutions.

These are the times when a lot of people fail because they give up because they find the obstacles they face to be too great to overcome. However, if you devote all of your energy to developing fresh ideas, success will follow.

Obsessing over your goals and overcommitting yourself won't stop you from achieving them, though. If you start scheduling more appointments and engaging in more conversations, you'll soon realize that your revenues are increasing by ten times.

Simply by deciding to fully dedicate yourself, your time, and your energy to accomplishing your goals, all of this may end up happening.

CHAPTER 6: TIME MANAGEMENT AND THE FEAR OF OVEREXPOSURE

How often do you find yourself doubting your ability to handle everything? It seems as though there aren't enough hours in the day as we rush around today finishing assignment after task. Time management is the answer that many people come up with; they figure out how to schedule their time to accomplish everything, right? For this reason, according to Cardone, time management is a myth: it's for those who don't think they can have it all.

In other words, Cardone thinks it's crucial to establish priorities in life, but that when you "manage" your time, you foster the idea that you can't have it all. On the other side, you won't need to strive to budget your time once you know that you can have everything you've ever wanted. Therefore, stop stating "I don't have enough time" and start making time instead. For instance, you could be doing something more productive with the time you waste at home watching TV or browsing the internet.

You'll need to find methods to do more with your time because you can't buy more of it. For instance, aim for ten emails each hour if you typically send five. In the same way, strive for fifteen phone calls if you only make five.

Set challenging objectives for yourself that will increase your productivity. Additionally, use this rule to your personal as well as your professional life. If you have kids, try to spend meaningful time with them whenever you can. Do something together instead of just watching TV. They will enjoy themselves more, and you will as well.

You'll discover how to spend your time more effectively and start experiencing success once you understand that you don't need to "control" it. It's natural that you will encounter criticism as you go along when this occurs. When you strive for omnipresence, you'll face even more criticism.

How does omnipresence work? Simply said, a corporation that is everywhere is well known. Many businesses have succeeded in their mission to be everywhere. McDonald's is a leader in the fast-food sector, and when it comes to social media, Facebook comes to mind. Everyone recognizes these companies, thus that ought to be your purpose.

You'll need to enhance your exposure, which requires a significant commitment, to reach omnipresence. Do not be concerned about customers losing patience with you or your business. If anything, your overexposure is working since those folks are aware of who you are and what kind of business you run. Keep moving forward and take whatever steps are necessary to continue spreading the word about yourself, whether it's setting up additional interviews or posting on social media.

CHAPTER 7: DEFINING SUCCESS AND IMPLEMENTING THE 10X RULE

Now that you know how to apply the 10X rule to your life, the final question is: how do you start on your journey to success?

Before you can answer this question, you must first decide what success means to you. Contrary to popular belief, it is impossible to determine someone's likelihood of success by looking at their family situation or level of schooling. Instead, success is a condition of mind.

In truth, successful people have a range of characteristics in common, but their "can-do" attitude is what distinguishes them. Your attitude toward challenges is one of the most significant qualities that could aid in your success. The response of successful people when faced with a challenge is "I'll figure it out." They explore outside the box and find a solution rather than assigning blame or adopting a victim attitude.

For instance, when it comes to customer satisfaction, effective people embrace that criticism and grow from it. They value criticisms and take the opportunity to improve.

Persistence is a trait shared by successful people. You'll never meet a successful person who gave up when things got difficult; rather, you'll find individuals who persisted despite all obstacles. Successful people are risk-takers, won't accept less-than-perfect results, and don't "earn" money. They also possess a persistence that will carry them forward. They instead create wealth.

So what is wealth then? Wealth encompasses more than just material possessions; it also includes ideas, beliefs, and things. For instance, you might use passive income from renting out your house to pay down your own mortgage! It is not possible to "make" money; all you have to do is know how to get it.

How then do you apply the 10X rule? Start by looking at successful people to determine what qualities they have that you don't. You should schedule your day such that you can rise earlier if they do get up earlier than you do. To spend meaningful time with his kid while his wife slept in, for instance, Cardone began rising an hour earlier after his daughter was born. If he got up an hour earlier, he could have it all. He didn't let his job suffer while he spent priceless time with his kid.

Create a list of your goals and put them in writing when you've decided what needs to change. Without worrying about how you will get there, just convince yourself that things will get done.

Make a list of the actions you must take to accomplish these goals, and then get to work! Take the early-morning step if it is essential. Make ten calls, publish on social media, and do everything else. Once you start carrying out your plans, you'll be well on your way to adhering to the 10X rule. Most importantly, persevere and stay motivated so that you can be successful.

CHAPTER 8: FINAL SUMMARY

Looking for outcomes that are ten times bigger than your current situation is the key to applying The 10X rule. You must put in 10 times as much effort as is anticipated to complete the task once you have outlined how to achieve it. Consider a reasonable goal and double it by ten, as underestimating one's talents is the most frequent mistake people make.

Change your focus, set greater goals than you think you can achieve, and then put in ten times as much effort as you think is necessary. You'll start to put in more effort, but you'll also start to achieve things you once thought were impossible.

If you have confidence in your abilities, a positive mindset, and put 100% of your effort into attaining your objectives, you'll see how the 10X strategy may improve your life.

ATOMIC HABITS

A habit is a behavior you automatically and automatically perform. like how a light switch automatically turns on when you walk into a dark room. You might not be cognizant of the influence a routine daily activity may have on your life. A dollar saved each day or a cigarette smoked each day may not seem like much now, but in 20 years, those actions might make you rich or, regrettably, put your life in jeopardy. It's important to understand how habits are formed in order to learn how to break bad habits and take back control of your life.

INTRODUCTION

If you're attempting to organize your life, Atomic Habits offers a straightforward foundation for daily development. James Clear, one of the world's leading experts on habit formation, provides guidance on how to create positive habits and break unhealthy ones.

You'll also learn how seemingly insignificant aspects of your daily routine can have a big impact on your life and your chances. If it's hard for you to break your habits, the problem is with your system, not with you.

You see, your brain is built to perform easy tasks with immediate rewards. James Clear, fortunately, provides a tried-and-true technique that will allow you to change your habit and enhance your quality of life.

This book will show you how to schedule time for new habits, overcome lack of motivation and willpower, build an environment that supports success, keep an eye on your actions, and find an accountability partner.

CHAPTER 1: WHY SMALL HABITS CAN MAKE A BIG DIFFERENCE

When it comes to success, a lot of individuals are focusing on the wrong thing. They believe that making crucial decisions will lead them there and place more importance on the final destination than the journey there. But this is the furthest thing from the truth there is.

In actuality, if you improve by 1% every day, you'll be 37 times better than you were yesterday; meanwhile, if you regress by 1% every day, you'll be so close to zero. In other words, it's the tiny things that matter and have the biggest influence.

For instance, a plane flying from Los Angeles to New York needs to be oriented precisely in the right direction to land there. Imagine that the pilot slightly changed the course of the aircraft by 3.5 degrees to the south.

The difference is so negligible that the average onlooker might not even notice it, making it appear to be nothing. Upon arrival, the passengers would undoubtedly notice a dramatic change. That minor course correction would change their final destination from New York to Washington, D.C.

Since little changes take time to take effect, they are typically not recognized. Although the consequences might not be felt for months or even years, they might still have a big impact.

Even though eating a slice of pizza every night for dinner won't necessarily make you unhealthy, you will undoubtedly notice a change in weight over the course of a year. Similar to this, going to a 30-minute yoga class one day won't instantaneously make you fit. Instead, it's modest actions compounded over time that have a cumulative impact.

Habits serve as a barometer for life outcomes.

Just like a person's net worth is just a reflection of their financial habits, a person's health may be decided by their daily eating and exercise habits. The difference between success and failure grows over time, so our daily choices have a greater impact than we may be aware of. If you want to predict where you will end up in life, just follow the path of your everyday choices.

Knowing how to set up your daily routines to work in your favor is essential because both poor and good habits can advance us. The key is to repeatedly practice little behavioral changes until they take the form of habits and produce noticeable results.

CHAPTER 2: HOW HABITS ARE FORMED

How many times have you begun a good habit—like working out or meditating—only to find that after a few days or weeks it has just become a significant burden?

Because so many people make unsuccessful attempts to change their behavior, habits may be hard to break. In order to change habits, we first need to understand how they are formed. The habit-forming process comprises four stages: trigger, desire, reaction, and reward.

Think about what you do when you first get in your car. You probably turn on your car, buckle up, check your mirrors, and then start driving. You just go through the motions without stopping to think. You have engaged in this conduct so frequently that it is now a reflex. Therefore, how do habits form? Habits begin with a signal or trigger that prompts them to act.

For instance, getting into your car signifies that you are ready to go on to your next destination. In this case, the desire to travel represents the second phase, which is the desire for a state shift. In response, you put your car in drive and accelerate. The final stage is the reward, which is a feeling of joy or relaxation from getting to your destination safely.

This habit loop can be used to implement many different daily rituals. for instance, brushing your teeth in the morning. Eating breakfast or drinking coffee may cause a desire to feel clean and fresh. Grab your toothbrush and head to the sink in the bathroom as your solution. Your reward is a mouth that feels clean and makes you feel prepared to face the day.

The cue always ignites a need, which is what triggers a response. Following the fulfillment of the desire, the reward is connected to the cue. The cue and craving stage of the habit loop is where our behaviors are driven by a desire to solve a particular problem. The buzzing of a new text message on your phone, for example, can serve as a sign that you are in the issue phase. The hunger is your desire to discover the knowledge in that message. The next step is the solution. You respond by picking up your phone and turning it on. The reward is the fulfillment of the urge to read the message.

These habits are certainly not all that bad, but when we form bad habits, we suffer the effects years later and find it more challenging to break the patterns. Understanding the habit loop is essential if you want to learn how to change your signals, wants, emotions, and incentives to develop healthy habits. Let's examine some methods you could begin forming better habits.

CHAPTER 3: MAKE IT OBVIOUS

When it comes to cues, we are reminded when our phone buzzes or when we drink coffee to check our messages or brush our teeth. However, once you are aware of how certain stimuli may impact our behavior, you may learn to manage your cues and develop better habits.

For instance, Anne Thorndike, a primary care physician at the Massachusetts General Hospital in Boston, believed that by just altering the environment, she could affect the eating habits of thousands of hospital staff members and visitors. She took the decision to substitute water bottles for soda in the refrigerators close to the cash register. Additionally, she provided bottled water for drinking at each station in the cafeteria. She didn't stop there. In comparison to soda sales, which fell by 11.4% percent over the course of three months, bottled water sales increased by 25.8%%. Since drinking water was more socially acceptable than pop, people altered their behavior to make better choices.

Humans, you see, possess the most powerful sense organ in the animal kingdom: eyesight. Of the almost eleven million sense receptors in the human body, only about ten million are specifically used for vision. In other words, visual cues are among the most powerful behavioral motivators. Therefore, even a small change in our perceptions could have a big effect on how we behave. Fortunately, we have the power to shape our environment. But how?

Imagine that you want to make playing the guitar a habit. You'll be much less likely to practice if you keep your guitar in a box in your closet. Instead, place your instrument in a prominent spot, such as the middle of the room.

If you want to eat healthily, snacks should be stored on the counter rather than concealed in the pantry. You'd like to work out more. Simply set your workout clothes and sneakers out the night before so you can see them when you get up.

Using visual cues may help you draw attention to your intended behavior. Additionally, you could generate the required signals by rehearsing your implementation objectives. Simply said, this means that you have a strategy for your actions, including when, where, and how you will carry them out.

Making a plan boosts your chances of keeping up your behaviors. According to a study of American voters, for instance, those who were asked "What time will you vote?" and "How will you get to the polling place?" were much more likely to vote than those who were merely asked "Will you vote?"

So instead of promising yourself that you will exercise more frequently, develop a plan and say, "On Monday, Wednesday, and Friday I'm going to go to spin class after work," and then pack a bag to bring to work and place it in the front seat of your car so that it is always in view!

CHAPTER 4: MAKE IT ATTRACTIVE

Daily advertising that promise to make everything more enticing, including clothing, food, and household goods, are all around us. Society is filled with highly doctored versions of reality because we tweak images with ideal lighting, photoshopped adjustments, and boosted features to make products more alluring and appealing to customers.

You could relate our actions to this. If something is more enticing to us, we are more likely to develop a habit of it.

You see, when we enjoy activities like eating or having sex, our brains release the feel-good hormone dopamine. We don't have to engage in these activities, though, because our brains also release dopamine when we imagine doing pleasurable tasks. Simply explained, this is our brain encouraging us to do something while rewarding us with a positive feeling.

Do you remember the excitement leading up to Christmas morning when you were a child? Children's brains create dopamine in anticipation of receiving gifts and seeing Santa, which drives them to associate happiness with Christmas.

Of course, not everything that makes us feel good is beneficial to our health. For instance, because they all make people feel good before and during the action, sex, drugs, and food are all easily addicted. But these addictions could harm our relationships and our health.

Because of this, it's crucial to capitalize on our knowledge when it comes to instilling positive behaviors. If we make doing something we enjoy a habit, we'll be more likely to follow through.

One strategy for achieving this is by bundling temptations. To make habits more tempting, temptation bundling combines an action you want to take with one you must perform. For instance, Ronan Byrne, a student of engineering from Ireland, felt he needed to exercise more but didn't want to.

a problem that many of us might relate to. Another thing we likely have in common is that Ronan like watching Netflix. His answer? He constructed a stationary bike and connected it to his laptop, but he wasn't content to pedal while watching Netflix nonstop. Instead, he developed a piece of software that limited Netflix playback to particular cycle speeds. In the end, he transformed a chore he loathed into a relationship with an enjoyable activity!

Even if Ronan had the knowledge to hack an exercise bike and create software to assist him bundle temptations, you don't need to be an engineer to follow this guidance to alter your own behaviour. It may be as easy as downloading your favorite shows to watch while running on the treadmill or rewarding yourself with a half-hour of Netflix after meeting certain work objectives to make your routines more enticing.

CHAPTER 5: MAKE IT EASY

Students in Jerry Uselmann's film photography class at the University of Florida were assigned a project that needed to be submitted at the end of the semester. He initially divided the class into two groups. The first group was advised that their mark would depend on how many photographs they submitted.

100 pictures, for instance, got an A, 90 got a B, 80 got a C, and so on. However, the grade for the second group would only be based on one photograph. Do you think the group that finished the semester with the higher grade is the number group? Then why? The quantity group was able to hone their skills because they created hundreds of photographs, but the quality group spent their time honing just one.

This concept can also be applied to our actions. People frequently take too much time pondering the best course of action and never take it. They might conduct research, develop strategies, and strategize, but they never carry out their plans. Therefore, rather than worrying about how long it would take to build a new habit, the key to mastering any behavior is to make it simple and easy to perform.

Many of us are motivated to carry out the humanly easy tasks. The more work it requires, the less likely we are to continue a habit. Of course, it may seem hard to simplify a difficult habit, but even the most difficult habits may be simplified using a variety of ideas and techniques!

Sending cards for occasions like birthdays, anniversaries, and condolences, for example, is a lovely habit to have, but the inconvenience of traveling to the store, selecting one, writing a message, and then mailing it makes us less likely to do it. The author's wife came up with a hack to make the act of mailing cards more practical. If the author and his wife buy a lot of cards and keep them around the house, they are much more likely to really send cards. People no longer had to exert themselves by going to the store to get cards because the process had been made simpler.

To stop dangerous behaviors, utilize this technique. The easiest way to do this is to make it impossible for the bad habit to persist. For instance, if you want to break the habit of watching TV after you come home from work, unhook the TV and take the batteries out of the remote. You'll be much more likely to spend your time creating a new, better habit than going to the trouble of turning on the TV.

Another method for making the creation of habits simple is the two-minute rule. The foundation of the rule is to start small and make the habit easy to start. Instead of telling yourself that you need to study for a class, you may start with the basics and tell yourself to "open my notes." Or perhaps you want to make it a habit to practice yoga after work.

Instead of reminding yourself, "I need to do yoga for thirty minutes," tell yourself to get your yoga mat out. By dividing a habit into manageable steps, you can make it easier to establish it, increasing your chance of establishing enduring habits.

CHAPTER 6: MAKE IT SATISFYING

The final step is to make the habit joyful. Successful firms are aware of this concept and apply it. For instance, toothpaste producers saw significant success when they incorporated mint into their formulations. People were able to enjoy brushing their teeth since mint gave off a nice, minty fresh sensation.

If an event wasn't satisfactory the first time, it can't be repeated.

In the 1990s, Stephen Luby worked as a public health expert in a region in Karachi. During his stay, Luby was able to reduce diarrhea among the local children by 52%. Additionally, by 48 percent and 35 percent, respectively, less people now have skin infections and pneumonia. How did he manage to do that? by using premium soap.

If you were up in a westernized setting, you are aware of the need of hand washing as a basic hygiene skill. Despite knowing this, the Pakistani neighborhood's people did not adopt the healthy habit of washing their hands. Luby collaborated with Proctor & Gamble to offer the neighborhood a premium soap that would make washing one's hands enjoyable.

Washing your hands seems to get more fun over night! Since the new soap lathered so well and smelled good, people started washing their hands regularly.

Like washing our hands or brushing our teeth, many other actions don't bring about the same immediate happiness. This is a circumstance of delayed reward. Even though we go to work every day, for instance, we might not get paid until the end of the month. Similar to this, it could take weeks or even months before you start noticing any advantages from weight loss or muscle toning, even if you start going to the gym every day.

On the other hand, actions that give immediate enjoyment could have unintended consequences. This is why smokers continue to do so even if they are aware of the risks that could lead to their demise. Cancer may not show its symptoms for 20 years, but in the meantime, it reduces stress and satisfies the desire for nicotine. Because of these delayed consequences and delayed advantages, it's critical to link desired behaviors to immediate fulfillment.

For instance, the author talks of his friends who wanted to cut back on eating out frequently in order to save money and improve their health. In order to accomplish this, they opened a savings account called "Trip to Europe" and deposited $50 in each time they skipped going out to eat. When they watched the money go into their savings, they immediately felt a sense of satisfaction, which encouraged them to keep doing it.

When they had enough money saved to make their habit satisfying and they could finally go on their trip, they immediately understood the long-term benefits.

CHAPTER 7: THE IMPORTANCE OF HABIT TRACKING

It might be difficult to form good habits or stop bad ones. While making progress is satisfying, the fulfillment is frequently delayed, which causes us to stop engaging in those healthy practices. Additionally, we don't always receive the desired external validation of our accomplishment while giving up bad habits like smoking. Fortunately, habit monitoring may be used to track your development objectively.

Habit monitoring is an easy yet effective tactic to make sure you are on track. But this strategy is not novel. When he was twenty, Benjamin Franklin started carrying a notebook everywhere he went. He truly kept an eye on his actions. Franklin kept a notebook where he recorded the instances in which he lived out his 13 core ideals. His virtues comprised both things he should do every day, like always do something positive, and things he should avoid, such engaging in pointless conversations. Franklin recorded his successes each night, creating a visual record of his positive behaviors.

Marking off days on a calendar as you go through your regular daily rituals is the easiest technique. You'll find that keeping track of your actions in a calendar or notepad increases your likelihood of keeping them up. Tracking is a good habit in addition to being obvious and giving you a visual depiction of your progress. You'll feel a sense of eagerness for when you've ended the day and accomplished everything you set out to do as you tick off each day. According to research, most people are more likely to succeed than those who do not track their advancement toward goals like losing weight, lowering blood pressure, and stopping smoking.

Additionally, if you employ a habit contract or have an accountability partner, things can change. Pleasurable experiences are more likely to be repeated than unpleasant or pricey ones, and both are more likely to be avoided. In other words, behavior adjusts when there is an instant repercussion. For instance, university students are more likely to show up to class if attendance affects their grades. Children go because they understand the consequences of not doing so. The same logic can be applied to encourage you to form healthy behaviors.

Bryan Harris, a businessman from Nashville, created a habit contract to hold him responsible for working out. He created a document that his wife and personal trainer had to sign requiring him to meet a 200-pound weight goal.

In order to achieve this goal, Bryan committed to weighing himself once a week and kept track of his food intake. He then put in place penalties for not doing these things. For instance, if he didn't keep track of his food intake, he would be required to pay his trainer $100 and his wife $500!

Bryan's habit contract was successful because, in addition to being concerned about losing the money, he cared about his wife's and trainer's thoughts.

He didn't want to disappoint them since knowing that someone was watching you can be enough motivation to succeed. This is why having an accountability partner or signing a habit contract can make it simpler to build good habits.

CHAPTER 8: FINAL SUMMARY

The things we do on a daily basis that have the most impacts on our lives are the tiny things, even though many people believe that making significant changes is the key to success. If we want to live long, happy lives, we must establish healthy habits because the individuals we become in the future will be shaped by our small, everyday actions today.

Naturally, given how tough it may be to form new habits, this is considerably more difficult to accomplish. Fortunately, there are several of methods available to help you create new behaviors right now. One of the four rules of habit building is to make things clear, appealing, simple, and gratifying. Making your routines satisfying, easy, and fun can improve your likelihood of sticking with them.

Additionally, it will be much easier to start new, healthy habits or break bad ones if you have a habit contract and an accountability partner.

CPSIA information can be obtained
at www.ICGtesting.com
Printed in the USA
LVHW081817261122
734044LV00013B/572

9 781944 237226